WILDFLOWERS, BUTTERFLIES & TREES
of the Slad Valley and the Cotswolds

RICHARD MORRIS

To Rosie, Grace and Annabelle

Many thanks to Rod Shaw and Shirley Mawer for their help and advice, and to John Spencer who assisted with editing and kindly provided three of the photographs.

I am indebted to Gloucestershire Wildlife Trust for checking the wildflower section.

ISBN: 978-0-9536339-6-8

Printed in Great Britain.

INTRODUCTION

Gloucestershire is rich in wild flowers and butterflies. This is partly because we still have some areas of unimproved limestone grassland, often on steep banks where wildlife can thrive.

I am lucky enough to live in a small hamlet called Elcombe in the Slad valley near Stroud.

Over the years I have struggled to remember the names of the many flora and fauna I have come across on my walks. I therefore decided to take photographs in order to help me with identification and to keep a record for the future.

I am not a professional photographer and would not claim to be an expert on flowers, butterflies or trees. So this book is aimed at the amateur enthusiast who enjoys walking and wants a simple coat-pocket size reference book. It is not a comprehensive list.

Often there is a single photo of a species. Sometimes there are two or more to help with identification or simply because it is particularly attractive. Most wild flowers have more than one 'common' name (and often several), so I decided to choose the one most frequently used in reference books.

The photographs of wildflowers are initially grouped by colour and then in alphabetical order. The butterfly and tree sections are in alphabetical order. Towards the end of the book there are some simple notes on trees, originally written for the children at the school where I taught.

CONTENTS

Greater Butterfly Orchid

WILD FLOWERS

Autumn Gentian

Autumn Gentian

Bittersweet

Bittersweet

Bluebell

Bluebell

Borage

Brooklime

Brooklime

Bugle

Bush Vetch

Clustered Bellflower

Clustered Bellflower

Columbine

Cornflower

Dame's Violet

Devil's-bit Scabious

Field Pansy

Field Scabious

Forget-me-not

Germander Speedwell

Grape Hyacinth

Green Alkanet

Ground Ivy

Harebell

Harebell

Ivy-leaved Speedwell

Ivy-leaved Speedwell

Ivy-leaved Toadflax

Ivy-leaved Toadflax

Lesser Burdock

Meadow Crane's-bill

Milkwort

Milkwort

Pasque Flower

Pasque Flower

Periwinkle (Greater)

Purple Toadflax

Selfheal

Selfheal

Small Scabious

Teasel

Tufted Vetch

Violet (Dog)

Violet (Dog)

Betony

Vipers Bugloss

Betony

Bistort

Bramble

Broadleaved Willowherb

Broadleaved Willowherb

Comfrey

Comfrey

Common Centaury

Common Fumitory

Common Knapweed

Common Poppy

Common Vetch

Creeping Thistle

Cuckoo Flower

Cut-leaved Germander

Deadly Nightshade

Dog Rose

Dove's-foot Cranesbill

Dove's-foot Cranesbill

Dwarf Mallow

Dwarf Thistle

Field Bindweed

Foxglove

Greater Knapweed

Greater Willowherb

Hedge Woundwort

Hedge Woundwort

Hemp Agrimony

Herb Robert

Honesty

Honesty

Honeysuckle

Indian Balsam

Marjoram

Marjoram

Marsh Thistle

Milkwort

Musk Mallow

Ragged Robin

Ragged Robin

Red Bartsia

Red Bartsia

Red Campion

Red Clover

Red Dead-nettle

Red Valerian

Redshank

Restharrow

Rosebay Willowherb

Rosebay Willowherb

Sainfoin

Salad Burnet

Scarlet Pimpernel

Shining Crane's-bill

Small-flowered Crane's-bill

Sorrel

Spear Thistle

Water Mint

Wild Basil

Wild Basil

Wild Thyme

Woolly Thistle

Wild Strawberry

Yarrow

Bladder Campion

Bittercress (hairy)

Bittercress (hairy)

Bramble

Burnet-Saxifrage

Burnet-saxifrage

Chickweed

Cleavers

Cow Parsley

Daisy

Enchanter's Nightshade

Enchanter's Nightshade

Eyebright

Fairy Flax

Garlic Mustard

Giant Hogweed

Greater Stitchwort

Ground Elder

Hedge Bedstraw

Hedge Bindweed

Hogweed

Honeysuckle

Ivy-leaved Speedwell

Ivy-leaved Toadflax

Ivy-leaved Toadflax

Knotgrass

Lily-of-the-valley

Meadowsweet

Mouse-ear

Ox-eye Daisy

Ramsons

Sanicle

Sanicle

Scentless Mayweed

Shepherd's Purse

Sweet Woodruff

Sweet Woodruff

Snowdrop

Watercress

Watercress

White Campion

White Clover

White Comfrey

White Dead-nettle

White Sweet Violet

Wild Angelica

Wild Carrot

Wood Anemone

Wood Sorrel

Wood Sorrel

Aconite

Yarrow

Agrimony

41

Beaked Hawksbeard

Beaked Hawkesbeard

Birds Foot Trefoil

Black Medick

Bulbous Buttercup

Bulbous Buttercup

Canadian Golden Rod

Charlock

Coltsfoot

Common Ragwort

Common Toadflax

Cowslip

Creeping Buttercup

Creeping Cinquefoil

Crosswort

Daffodil (cultivated)

Dandelion

Dyer's Greenweed

Dyer's Greenweed

Evening Primrose

Fennel

Fox and Cubs

Goat's-beard

Goldilocks Buttercup

Great Mullein

Greater Celandine

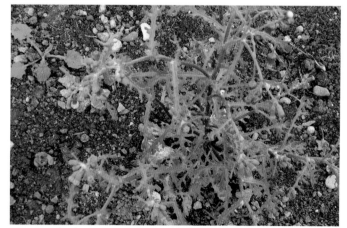

Groundsel

Groundsel

Hawks-beard

Hawkweed

Hawkweed

Hedge Mustard

Hop Trefoil

Horseshoe Vetch

Kidney Vetch

Lady's Bedstraw

Lesser Celandine

Lesser Trefoil

Marsh Marigold

Meadow Buttercup

Meadow Vetchling

Monkey Flower

Mouse-ear Hawkweed

Nipplewort

Pineapple Weed

Ploughmans Spikenard

Primrose

Rock Rose

Silverweed

Smooth Sow-thistle

St John's-wort

Tutsan

Wall Lettuce

Welsh Poppy

Wood Avens

Yellow Archangel

Yellow Corydalis

Yellow Flag

Yellow Oxalis

Yellow Rattle

Yellow Wort

Carline Thistle

Black Bryony

Carline Thistle

Common Orache

Common Sorrel

Common Stinging Nettle

Cuckoo Pint

Curled Dock

Dog's Mercury

Dog's Mercury

Gooseberry

Herb Paris

Horse Tails

Ivy

Pellitory-of-the-wall

Plantain Hoary

Plantain Ribwort

Traveller's Joy

White Bryony

Wood Sage

Wood Spurge

ORCHIDS

Autumn Lady's Tresses

Bee Orchid

Bee Orchid

Bird's Nest Orchid

Broad-leaved Heleborine

Broad-leaved Heleborine

Common Spotted Orchid

Common Spotted Orchid

Early Purple Orchid

Early Purple Orchid

Fly Orchid

Fly Orchid

Fragrant Orchid

Fragrant Orchid

Frog Orchid

Greater Butterfly Orchid

Greater Butterfly Orchid

Green-winged Orchid

Lesser Butterfly Orchid

Musk Orchid

Pyramidal Orchid

Pyramidal Orchid

Twayblade

White Helleborine

BUTTERFLIES

Adonis Blue

Adonis Blue

Brimstone (male)

Brown Argus

Brown Argus

Chalkhill Blue (male)

Chalkhill Blues

Comma

Comma

Common Blue (female)

Common Blue (male)

Common Blues

Dark Green Fritillary

Dingy Skipper

Dingy Skipper

Duke of Burgundy eggs

Duke of Burgundy (male)

Gatekeeper (female)

Gatekeeper (male)

Gatekeeper

Green Hairstreak

Green Veined White (female)

Green Veined White (male)

Holly Blue (female)

Holly Blue (male)

Large Blue Egg

Large Blue (female)

Large Blue (male)

Large Blues

Large Skipper

Large White eggs

Large White

Marble White (male)

Marble Whites

Marsh Fritillary

Marsh Fritillary

Meadow Brown (female)

Meadow Brown (male)

Meadow Brown (underside)

Orange Tip eggs on Cuckoo Flower

Orange Tip (male)

Orange Tip

Painted Lady

Painted Lady

83

Peacock

Pearl-bordered Fritillary

Pearl-bordered Fritillary

Red Admiral

Red Admiral

Ringlet

Ringlet

Silver-washed Fritillary (Valenzina)

Silver-washed Fritillary (male) - underside

Silver-washed Fritillary (male)

Small Blue (female)

Small Blue (male)

Small Blue

Small Blues

Small Copper

Small Copper

Small Heath

Small Heath

Small Skipper

Small Skipper

Small White

Speckled Wood

Speckled Wood

Small Tortoiseshell

DAY-FLYING MOTHS

Burnet Companions

Cinnabar

Cistus Forester

Grass Rivulet

Common Heath

Common Heath

Green Longhorn

Hummingbird Hawkmoth

Mother Shipton

Pyrausta Nigrata

Pyrausta Nigrata

Pyrausta Purpuralis

Ruby Tiger

Scarlet Tiger

Scarlet Tigers

Silver Y

Six-spot Burnet

Six-spot Burnets

Small Purple-barred

Yellow Shell

GRASSES

Upright
Brome

Meadow-grass

Crested
Dogstail

Quaking
Grass

97

Yorkshire
Fog

Wood
Melick

Sweet
Vernal

False
Oat-grass

Cocksfoot

Ryegrass

Barren
Brome

Soft
Brome

99

Cats
Tail

Tor-grass

Annual
Meadow-grass

Barley-grass

TREES & SHRUBS

TREE INFORMATION

There are two million hectares (about the size of Wales) of woodland in the United Kingdom.

There are thirty three native tree species. Of these, three are conifers - Scots Pine, Yew and Juniper. The rest are described as broadleaved. Most broadleaved trees are deciduous and most conifers are evergreen.

Trees are a huge 'sink' for carbon dioxide - so may reduce the effect of global warming. Carbon dioxide from the air and water from the soil is used by plants to make their food.

There is as much of a tree below the ground as there is above. Trees are a habitat for a wide range of animals.

ASH

One of the last trees to come into leaf in the spring. It has an open canopy, so some sunlight can penetrate the ground beneath - resulting in rich plant and invertebrate life.

The wood is good for furniture, tool handles and for making arrows. It can be burned green (freshly cut) and is often used in woodburning stoves.

BEECH

A magnificent tree which grows well in the Cotswolds. It has dense foliage so little plant life grows under it. It produces small nuts called 'mast'.

Due to its shallow roots it may be vulnerable to the effects of 'global warming'. Excellent for making furniture.

CHERRY *(Wild)*

Cherry trees can be recognised by the horizontal bands on the trunk. They have white blossom and the seeds are spread by birds.

Used for furniture and carving.

GINKGO

Often used in parks and gardens in the United Kingdom, but native to China. It is one of the oldest tree species known - 250 million year old fossils have been found.

HAZEL

Used to be very important for coppicing - cut every seven years for sheep hurdles, fencing and bean sticks. The nuts (or cobs) are good to eat and are high in protein.

HOLLY

Holly trees are either male or female - if it has winter berries then the tree is female. The leaves are waxy to prevent water loss in winter. The prickles prevent grazing by deer - there are fewer prickles higher up the tree because the deer can't reach.

In pre-Christian times holly was used as a winter decoration, but in the Middle Ages the berries and spikes were linked to the Crucifixion.

HORSE CHESTNUT *(Conker Tree)*

Legend has it that originally conkers were called conquerors. In times of war during the 16th century, the Turks in Constantinople fed conkers to their sick horses. During battle it was vital to have strong horses in order to conquer your enemy.

In the spring the spectacular flowers resemble candles. The wood can be used for carving.

LARCH

The Larch is a deciduous conifer. It was introduced from Europe in the 17th century. Like all conifers it produces cones which contain seeds.

The wood is mostly used for building materials and fences on farms.

LIME

Lime trees are often grown in parklands and towns because of their attractive foliage. However, they can produce sideshoots from the base of the trunk and also attract aphids which excrete honeydew.

The wood is good for carving. The lime tree has nothing to do with the fruit lime, or indeed limestone.

OAK

Oaks can grow anywhere but do best on fertile soils. In the autumn they produce acorns, which used to be grazed by pigs. A large tree can take up to a tonne of water a day from the soil.

In the 18th century it took 3000 oak trees to build a Man-of-war fighting ship. The oldest oak in England is about 800 years old.

POPLAR

These tall, elegant trees have leaves which quiver in the slightest breeze. They must not be grown near houses because the roots take up lots of water. The wood can be used as biofuel and plywood.

ROBINIA

An attractive ornamental tree of the same family as peas and beans. It has pretty white flowers in the Spring, and pods in the autumn. It is a native of the Eastern USA.

SCOTS PINE

This tree used to grow wild throughout the United Kingdom, but is now mostly limited to the Scottish Highlands. It has needles instead of broad leaves and produces separate male and female flowers. The seeds are spread by cones.

SILVER BIRCH

Often planted in gardens and parks because of its attractive silver bark. In young replanted woodland it is considered a weed tree. It is also susceptible to fungal attack. It has a short lifespan (about 60 years) and limited use.

SWEET CHESTNUT

Introduced by the Romans about 2000 years ago to make flour called 'pollenta' from the nuts. This was a staple ration for the Roman legions.

It is long lived (maximum 500 years). An attractive ornamental tree, although the wood can only be used for fencing etc.

SYCAMORE

Introduced from France in the Middle Ages, and one of the Maple family. The fruits are the wings containing the seeds. They spin like helicopters to take the seed away from the parent plant.
Used for furniture, flooring, carving and violins.

WELLINGTONIA

A Redwood, discovered by John Bidwell (in California) in 1853, a year after the Duke of Wellington died.

The world's biggest tree is a Redwood growing in California. It is 4000 years old, weighs 1000 tonnes and has a girth of 23 metres. The thick air-filled bark (a good thermal insulator) protects it against forest fires.

YEW

An evergreen tree with poisonous foliage and seeds. The seeds are spread by birds which digest the fruit while the seed passes through them.

They are often found in churchyards, as it used to be thought that they warded off evil spirits.

The oldest known Yew tree is in Scotland, and thought to be 4000 years old. The tallest Yew hedge is in Cirencester.

Alder

Alder

Ash

Ash

Aspen

Beech

Beech

Blackthorn

Blackthorn

Buddleia

Cherry

Cherry

Cherry Laurel

Cherry Laurel

Copper Beech

Copper Beech

Dogwood

Dogwood

Elder

Elder

Elm (English)

Elm (English)

Field Maple

Field Maple

Guelder-rose

Hawthorn

Hazel

Hazel

Holly

Holly

Hornbeam

Hornbeam

Horse Chestnut

Horse Chestnut

Juniper

Juniper

Larch

Larch

Lime

Lime

Maple

Oak (English)

Oak (English)

Oak (Holm)

Oak (Holm)

Poplar

Poplar

Privet

119

Robinia

Robinia

Rowan

Rowan

Scots Pine

Scots Pine

Silver Birch

Silver Birch

Spindle

Spindle fruit

Sweet Chestnut

Sweet Chestnut

Sycamore

Sycamore

Walnut

Wayfaring

Whitebeam

Whitebeam

Wild Service

Wild Service

Willow

Willow

Yew

Yew

125

NOTES: